Space-ology

Becoming an
ASTRONAUT

by Ellen Lawrence

Consultant:
Josh Barker
Space Communications Team
National Space Centre
Leicester, United Kingdom

BEARPORT
PUBLISHING

New York, New York

Credits

Cover, © AFP/Getty Images; 4, © Andrey Armyagov/Shutterstock; 5, © ESA; 6, © NASA; 7, © NASA; 8, © ESA; 9, © ESA; 10, © Bill Ingalls/NASA; II, © NG Images/Alamy; 12, © Military Collection/Alamy; 13, © Paul Hakimata/Dreamstime; 14T, © V. Crubo/ESA; 14B, © ESA; 15, © ESA; 16, © NASA; 17, © ESA; 18, © NASA/Alamy; 19, © H. Rueb/ESA; 20, © S. Corvaja/ESA; 21, © ITAR-TASS News Agency/Alamy; 23TL, © Vibrant Pictures/Alamy; 23TC, © Chutima Chaochaiya/Shutterstock; 23TR, © NASA; 23BL, © ESA; 23BC, © BlueRingMedia/Shutterstock; 23BR, © Military Collection/Alamy.

Publisher: Kenn Goin
Senior Editor: Joyce Tavolacci
Creative Director: Spencer Brinker
Photo Researcher: Ruth Owen Books

Library of Congress Cataloging-in-Publication Data

Names: Lawrence, Ellen, 1967– author.
Title: Becoming an astronaut / by Ellen Lawrence.
Description: New York, New York : Bearport Publishing, [2019] | Series:
 Space-ology | Includes bibliographical references
 and index.
Identifiers: LCCN 2018050776 (print) | LCCN 2018052098 (ebook) |
ISBN 9781642802436 (ebook) | ISBN 9781642801743 (library)
Subjects: LCSH: Astronauts—Training of—Juvenile literature. | Manned space
 flight—Juvenile literature.
Classification: LCC TL793 (ebook) | LCC TL793 .L29945 2019 (print) | DDC
 629.45/07—dc23
LC record available at https://lccn.loc.gov/2018050776

For more information, write to Bearport Publishing Company, Inc., 45 West 21st Street, Suite 3B, New York, New York 10010. Printed in the United States of America.

13 12 11 10 9 8 7 6 5 4 3 2

Contents

Danger!........................... 4

Astronauts Wanted............. 6

Basic Training 8

Learning to Fly 10

A Space Station on Earth 12

"Cavenauts" 14

The Vomit Comet............. 16

A Walk in Space.............. 18

Blast Off! 20

Science Lab 22

Science Words 23

Index 24

Read More 24

Learn More Online 24

About the Author 24

Danger!

A spacecraft hurtles through space.

Suddenly, lights flash and alarms ring as smoke fills the **cockpit**.

The astronauts inside have just seconds to decide what to do.

Thankfully, the spacecraft is a simulator and is not actually on fire.

The astronauts are taking part in a training exercise on Earth!

Soyuz spacecraft

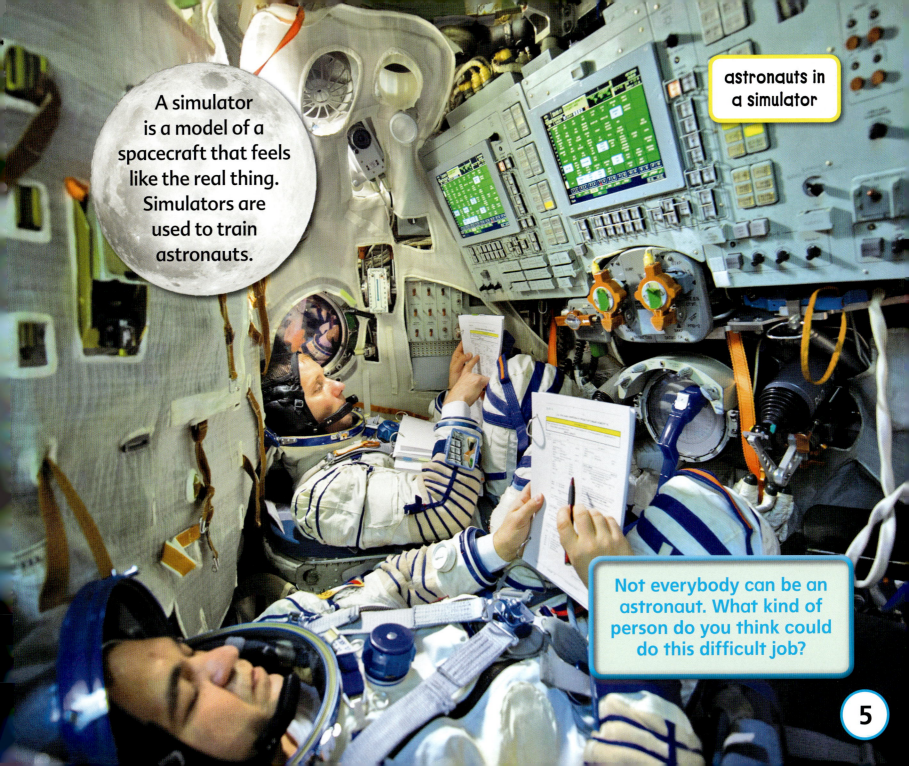

A simulator is a model of a spacecraft that feels like the real thing. Simulators are used to train astronauts.

astronauts in a simulator

Not everybody can be an astronaut. What kind of person do you think could do this difficult job?

Astronauts Wanted

Only people with special skills can become astronauts.

Many have worked as pilots, scientists, or **engineers**.

First, they apply to a space agency such as NASA (National Aeronautics and Space Administration).

If they are chosen, they will train to work on the International Space Station (ISS) or for other space missions!

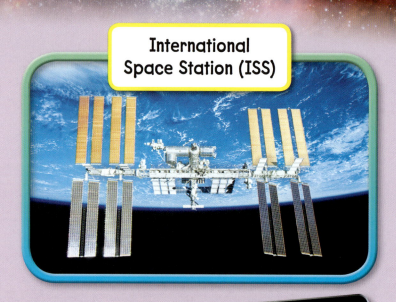

International Space Station (ISS)

ASTRONAUT CHECKLIST

An astronaut must:
- ✓ Be in great health
- ✓ Have excellent eyesight
- ✓ Be good at math and science
- ✓ Have a good memory
- ✓ Be calm in difficult or scary situations
- ✓ Be unafraid of heights and small cramped spaces

NASA's 2017 trainee astronauts take a selfie.

Thousands of people apply to NASA, but only a few become astronauts. The 12 trainees chosen in 2017 beat 18,300 other people!

Basic Training

Once people are selected to become astronauts, they begin basic training.

They learn how to fly the Soyuz and other spacecraft to the ISS.

They must learn how to repair all the equipment if something breaks.

Trainees are also taught basic medical skills, such as how to give a shot.

To make sure they've learned everything, they take hundreds of tests.

These trainees are practicing fixing the ISS toilet!

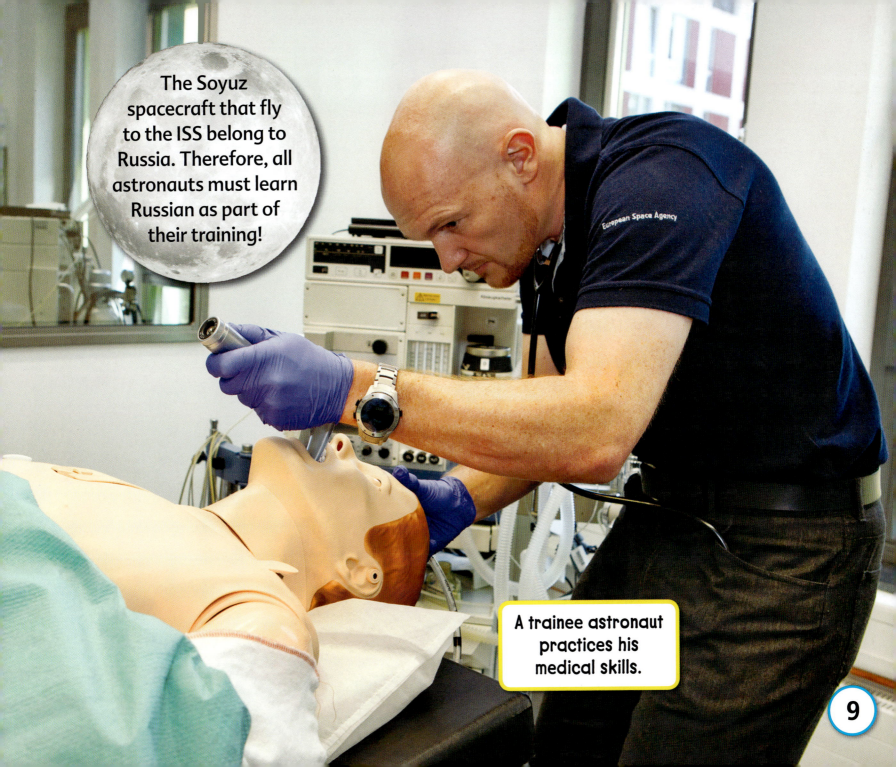

The Soyuz spacecraft that fly to the ISS belong to Russia. Therefore, all astronauts must learn Russian as part of their training!

A trainee astronaut practices his medical skills.

9

Learning to Fly

Flying a spacecraft is extremely difficult and dangerous.

Astronauts practice every maneuver for hundreds of hours in a simulator.

They work on taking off, **orbiting** Earth, and connecting to the ISS.

It's a little like playing a very complicated video game.

However, the crew knows that a single mistake could mean disaster.

Soyuz simulator

an astronaut training inside a Soyuz simulator

A simulator can be programmed to create an emergency. This helps the trainees learn how to solve problems under pressure.

A Space Station on Earth

Trainee astronauts also spend time in a life-size model of the ISS.

They prepare for the **experiments** they will carry out in space.

They also learn how every part of the space station works.

Each astronaut must know how to fix hundreds of machines.

Astronauts also train using **virtual reality** (VR). They wear VR headsets that allow them to see the space station all around them. They practice carrying out tasks.

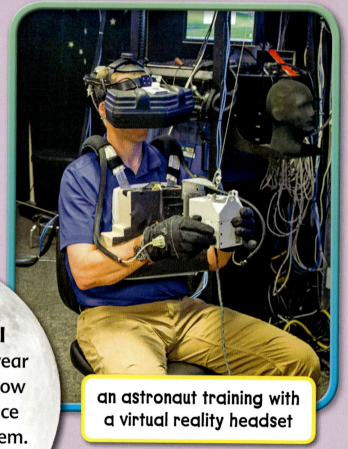

an astronaut training with a virtual reality headset

a life-size model of the ISS

"Cavenauts"

To prepare for life in space, trainee astronauts spend a week in a cave!

Deep underground, there is no day or night—just like in space.

The trainees have only a limited amount of food and water.

They must explore the cave and work as a team to complete a mission.

The mission might be to collect samples of gases and rocks, or to look for signs of life.

a trainee doing an experiment

trainees eating lunch underground

Like space, a cave is a dark, dangerous place to work. The trainee astronauts learn to rely on each other.

The trainee astronauts are known as "cavenauts." Here, they're setting up camp.

15

The Vomit Comet

To be ready to live in space, astronauts must experience weightlessness.

On Earth, **gravity** pulls everything toward the ground.

Inside a spacecraft or space station, astronauts feel weightless.

To learn how this feels, trainees fly on a plane known as the Vomit Comet.

First, the plane flies high into the sky, then it dives toward Earth, creating the effect trainees will feel in space.

The Vomit Comet earned its name because it makes some trainees feel very sick.

Inside the Vomit Comet, the astronauts practice moving while weightless. They even try running on a treadmill!

You may have seen astronauts floating in the ISS on TV. What do you think is the most difficult thing to do while weightless?

A Walk in Space

Astronauts also prepare for space walks, or EVAs (Extra-Vehicular Activities).

They train in a giant swimming pool that contains a model of the ISS.

In the water, astronauts practice using special tools.

They also learn to use tethers to connect themselves to the ISS.

Without a tether in space, an astronaut could float away and die.

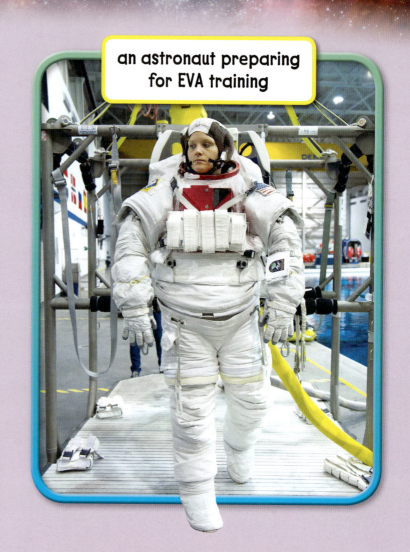

an astronaut preparing for EVA training

During a practice EVA, an astronaut wears an air-filled suit and a heavy belt. The suit makes the trainee float and the belt makes him or her sink. This causes the astronaut to feel weightless—just like in zero gravity!

tether

trainee astronaut

19

Blast Off!

Finally, after six years of training, the big day arrives.

Five, four, three, two, one . . . liftoff!

A newly trained astronaut blasts into space.

In just six hours, the Soyuz spacecraft will reach the ISS.

Then, it will be time to do one of the world's most exciting jobs.

These astronauts are about to board a Soyuz spacecraft.

The word *astronaut* comes from the Greek words *astron* and *nautes*, which mean "star" and "sailor."

Which part of becoming an astronaut do you think is the hardest? Which part is the most fun?

21

Science Lab

Think Like an Astronaut!

Astronauts must be able to concentrate and think fast. Try this test to discover if you can think like an astronaut.

> **You will need:**
> - A notebook
> - A friend to help you
> - A timer
> - Colored pencils or markers

To complete the test, you must look at the words and say the color of each word, *not* the word that's written. For example:

BLUE

You must say "red."

When you're ready to start, ask your friend to time you. Read from left to right. If you make a mistake, you must start again!

How quickly can you finish the test without making a mistake?

BLUE	RED
GREEN	BLUE
PURPLE	YELLOW
ORANGE	BLUE
RED	GREEN
PURPLE	YELLOW

Now try writing your own set of 12 color words and test your friend. Can he or she beat your time?

Science Words

cockpit (KOK-pit) the area of a plane or spacecraft where the pilot sits

engineers (en-juh-NIHRZ) people who are trained to design, build, and repair machines or structures

experiments (ek-SPER-uh-ments) scientific tests set up to find the answer to a question

gravity (GRAV-uh-tee) the force that pulls things toward Earth

orbiting (OR-bit-ing) circling, or moving around, another object

virtual reality (VUR-choo-uhl ree-AL-uh-tee) an environment created by computers that looks real

Index

basic training 8
"cavenauts" 14–15
International Space
   Station (ISS) 6, 8–9,
   10, 12–13, 18, 20

medical training 8–9
NASA 6–7
simulators 4–5, 10–11
Soyuz spacecraft 8–9,
   10–11, 20

space walks 18–19
virtual reality (VR) 12
Vomit Comet 16–17
weightlessness 16–17, 19

Read More

Lawrence, Ellen. *Surviving in Space (Space-ology).* New York: Bearport (2019).

Rustad, Martha E. H. *Becoming an Astronaut (An Astronaut's Life).* North Mankato, MN: Capstone (2018).

Shirley, Rebekah Joy. *I Want to Be an Astronaut (Let's Play Dress Up).* New York: Rosen (2012).

Learn More Online

To learn more about astronaut training, visit
www.bearportpublishing.com/space-ology

About the Author

Ellen Lawrence lives in the United Kingdom and fully admits to being a huge space geek! While researching and writing this series, she loved watching interviews with astronauts and spine-tingling launch countdowns.